DS

his

D1139572

orfolk.gov.uk/libraries or

).

HAUS CURIOSITIES

Citizens of Everywhere

About the Author

Peter Gumbel is a Paris-based writer and editor. He has worked for US publications including the *Wall Street Journal*, *Time*, and *Fortune*. He is the author of a best-selling book on French education, *On achève bien les écoliers* (*They Shoot School Kids, Don't They?*), published by Grasset in 2010.

Peter Gumbel

CITIZENS OF EVERYWHERE

Searching for Identity in the Age of Brexit

First published by Haus Publishing in 2020
4 Cinnamon Row
London SW11 3TW
www.hauspublishing.com

Copyright © 2020 Peter Gumbel

The right of the author to be identified as the author of this work has been asserted in accordance with the Copyright, Designs and Patents Act 1988

A CIP catalogue record for this book is available from the British Library

Print ISBN: 978-1-913368-07-4
Ebook ISBN: 978-1-913368-08-1

Typeset in Garamond by MacGuru Ltd

Printed in Czech Republic

All rights reserved

Contents

Acknowledgements

I am grateful to Barbara Schwepcke for her abiding interest in my family and thank the team at Haus Publishing for the speed, skill, and delicacy with which they turned my manuscript into this book.

My beloved daughters Sofia and Olivia, for whom this essay was originally conceived, are enthusiastic readers and astute editors, among their other talents. I thank them for suggesting examples to include and pointing to redundant phrases, faulty logic, and half-baked ideas that needed fixing.

My heartfelt thanks go also to Sylvie Godron, who provided unwavering support and nudged me to draw broader conclusions about the values that truly matter; John Ziaukas and Loren Segan, who gave extensive feedback on multiple drafts and encouraged me to dig deeper into my own feelings; Ellen-Marion Huss in Cottbus, who handed me a treasure trove of documents that filled blank spots in my grandparents' story; and Judith Friedlaender, who piqued my curiosity about acquiring a German passport in the first place and shared revealing correspondence between her father and mine.

The journey I describe in this essay is a personal one, but it is not one I have undertaken alone. Many people have helped me along the way, from university friends to hiking and poker buddies and work colleagues in Britain, France, Germany, and the United States. I have been inspired by conversations with my sisters and brothers about our common heritage. My late godmother Joan Rubinstein opened many doors in my thinking. I owe the largest debt of gratitude to my parents Ellen and Edward, my aunt Marion, my grandmothers Carla and Elizabeth, and the uncle and grandfathers I never knew, Maxi, Ernst, and Gustav. They would be heartbroken to see Britain turning its back on Europe, and yet they were survivors who were able to adapt. I salute their resilience – and dedicate this essay to their memory.

Prologue: Mobility and National Identity in a Time of Plague

On a sunny Tuesday morning in September 2019, my elder daughter and I walked into the German consulate in Paris with our British passports and re-emerged fifteen minutes later as German citizens. History had come full circle: eighty years and six months earlier, in March 1939, my maternal grandparents fled Nazi Germany after months of increasingly desperate efforts to leave the country. They got out just before the borders closed and went to England, which they viewed as a bastion of freedom and safety. Stripped of their German nationality, they remained stateless until 1946, when they became naturalised British citizens.

Compared with their history, obtaining our German naturalisation certificates was a formality devoid of all drama. It took just a signature, a photocopy, and a handshake – but it felt momentous nonetheless. If anybody had told me even a few years previously that I would apply to become German, I would have been incredulous. But times change, and circumstances change with them. After the 2016 Brexit referendum, several members of my family (all of whom were born in Great Britain) chose to apply for German citizenship as an insurance policy in the event that Britain's withdrawal from the European Union should turn out badly. It's an irony of history that a Nazi decree from November 1941 revoking the citizenship of German Jews who had left the country gave us the opening we needed: an article of the postwar German constitution stipulates that descendants of Germans who "were deprived of their citizenship on political, racial, or religious grounds shall on application have their citizenship restored".[1] So we applied.

We are not alone. After the referendum, several thousand British families with German–Jewish backgrounds did the same. I risked having to contend with a welter of bureaucracy to continue living and working in Paris as a British citizen post-Brexit. Connecting with my historic roots in this way was more than just pragmatism, though. Brexit challenged the essence of my identity, and so I made a conscious choice to become German. British by birth, I am European by conviction and heritage, and now I have an unambiguous European nationality to prove it.

This essay is largely a personal story: my reflections on becoming German and closing the cycle of history after fourscore years. The Covid-19 pandemic broke out while I was writing and, though it is not related to my family history, that crisis provided a different context and new evidence to validate two of the broader points I make in the following pages. They are, firstly, the paramount need to defend our freedom of movement across borders, which is all the more precious for being relatively recent, and, secondly, the waning relevance of national identity itself. Even before the virus struck, both of these ideas ran counter to the prevailing political mood in the United Kingdom, the United States, and a growing number of other countries. But in its perverse way, Covid-19 brought home just how important it is to defend and propagate these principles. The pandemic exposed the limitations of political geography: here was a disease that knew no borders, respected no jurisdictions, and infected people regardless of the colour of their passport. It also exposed the inadequacy of the nation-first reflex to ward off this "invisible enemy".

The crisis thus serves as a reminder of how our societies have been stricken by a different kind of sickness that, in many ways, is worse than the novel coronavirus. This other disease is the delusion of national exceptionalism, and its main symptom is a rejection of everything and everyone that fails to fit into its stifling us-versus-them world view. An earlier strain of that delusional malady nearly killed my grandparents and wiped out our family eighty years ago. All the more reason to take a stand against it today.

1

Exile, or the Perilous Illusion of Belonging

All four of my grandparents were proud German citizens until the Nazis decreed that they were not German at all but members of an inferior race that needed to be eradicated. On both sides of my family, the implications of this violent undermining of their identity took a long time to sink in and even longer to act upon, until it was almost too late. The consequences, both physical and psychological, were traumatic. Even today, among later generations, the idea that we may not fully "fit in" remains a family demon.

Most of the history I recount in this essay concerns my mother's side of the family. This is because I possess detailed correspondence documenting some of the ordeals her parents experienced during the Third Reich. After my maternal grandmother's death in 1989, I found carbon copies of letters her husband had written fifty years previously. These letters trace their flight from Germany and arrival in England. As well as a record of dates and names, the correspondence provides precious glimpses of the emotion they felt. On my father's side, by contrast, the only first-hand documentation available is almost entirely from my father's own memoirs, which are filtered through his upbeat personality and coloured by time; he experienced Hitler's accession to power in January 1933 as a law student in Berlin and left Germany three months later. He went on to study in Zurich and London and only put pen to paper six decades later.

Both sides of my family had ample reason to see themselves as German through and through. In their respective local communities, they were well established and evidently respected. My father's father, Gustav Gümbel, started his career in the family wine business before opening a bank in the Rhineland town of Bingen. Family lore has it that he faced down a mob of political radicals who threatened to storm the bank in the chaotic aftermath of the French march into the Ruhr in 1923. A few years later, his bank was acquired by Deutsche Bank, and he then served as president of the regional Chamber of Commerce and Industry until he was forced to resign after Hitler took power. Even so, as late as July 1934, he was decorated for his wartime service, having been wounded in a road accident during the First World War. That same year, he and my grandmother decided to build themselves a new house on a plot of land they had acquired in Bingen – not the sort of decision you would take if you had any doubt about your longer-term prospects.

On my mother's side, the family pedigree and rootedness in the local community was even stronger. My great-grandfather Max Grünebaum was an entrepreneur who moved from the family home in Lippstadt to the town of Cottbus, about eighty miles southeast of Berlin, in 1872. At the time, Cottbus was a thriving hub of the German textile industry and Max began work in a cloth mill. Four years later, he and a brother-in-law set up their own company. Demand soared across Europe for the high-quality worsted yarn the factory produced, and it was quickly riding the powerful industrialisation and export wave of those years. Max made a fortune and eventually bought out his partner. He built himself a sumptuous villa in the centre of Cottbus. Not content with just leading a comfortable life, he became socially and politically active. With his wife Caroline, he created a pension fund for his employees and set up a foundation that gave grants to the local children's hospital to combat scarlet fever. He financed city parks and a riverside promenade.[2] Together with other affluent families, he also supported the construction of a magnificent Art Deco theatre, which still stands, and for which his factory wove the first curtain. He was recognised for his civic activities in October 1908, when Cottbus awarded him the freedom of the city. Five months later, in March 1909, Kaiser Wilhelm bestowed on him the honorary title of *Kommerzienrat* – commercial counsellor. He was active in local municipal politics for three decades and, during the First World War, stepped in to serve as acting mayor. By then he was in his early sixties.

The high standing in which both families were held probably contributed to a false sense of security once Hitler came to power. How could such pillars of the local community be at risk? Both great-grandfathers were luminaries in their respective local Jewish communities. The entrepreneurial Max Grünebaum served for a time as a board member of the Cottbus synagogue. On his death in 1925, the synagogue published a notice in the local newspaper that lauded him for "openly professing his Jewish faith throughout his life". On my father's side, too, the family gave financial support to the Bingen synagogue. Yet several family members had severed their ties to Judaism long before the Nazis took power. They included my maternal grandmother Carla, who had converted to Christianity more than two decades previously; among her papers, I found her certificate of baptism into the Protestant church, dated February 1910. Her husband, Ernst, converted in January 1923. My father, too, was deeply ambiguous about his Jewish roots. In a family memoir published privately before he died in 1995, he wrote: "As a family, we tended to look upon our Jewish heritage as a legacy of the past which would continue to recede but had lost most, if not all, of its social as well as its spiritual hold."

This shifting relationship with Judaism is not atypical. Some academic studies have noted a general tendency at that time among bourgeois Jewish families in Germany to assimilate; one theory is that they wanted to differentiate themselves from the *shtetl* Jews in Eastern Europe whom they viewed as less affluent, less integrated, and less cultured.[3] My family papers contain no trace of an explanation about the intergenerational shift in faith other than a brief reference by my father in his memoir: "Curious as it may sound, there was even a whiff of anti-Semitism in the air at our home. We sensed that after a thousand years of ghetto life in towns and cities, it was time to escape from it into a larger, more open, more outward-directed world with wider interests, different values, and new ideals."

While my grandparents saw themselves as thoroughly German, to the Nazis they were Jews. Conversion to Christianity was no help, and local churches simply fell into line with that racial logic. In December 1938, the Cottbus Protestant church wrote to my grandmother informing her that, despite more than a quarter century of active membership, the local synod had unanimously voted to reject her annual dues and was refunding the instalment she had already paid. In other words, she was being kicked out of the church.

That episode was just one indication of how Ernst and Carla's once comfortable world was collapsing around them. Humiliations became part of their daily experience. They were obliged by law to add "Israel" and "Sara" to their official names at the city registry office; they initially ignored the police order to do so but responded to the second warning with a curt letter saying that they had complied. They had to surrender their passports, which meant Ernst could no longer leave Germany to meet international clients, and they were obliged to fire their maid, Käthe, because of the Nazi race laws; she was deemed to be Aryan and thus not allowed to work for people who weren't. My grandparents found her a new employer, but she was so eager to remain with them that she lodged a request with the local labour office for special dispensation to stay on. The police promptly called her in for questioning. The minutes of her deposition, housed in the city archives, suggest that they peppered her with questions about the family, including insidious ones about whether Ernst had ever shown signs of "immoral" behaviour. She insisted that they were model employers, but her request to continue working for them was nonetheless denied.

My grandparents finally saw the writing on the wall and started to respond. In the spring of 1937, they sent their sixteen-year-old twin daughters – my mother Ellen and aunt Marion – to a boarding school in Switzerland. Less than eighteen months later, they entrusted their son into the hands of Quakers promising to spirit him out of the country by train and boat to a destination yet to be determined, but most likely Canada. Once the children had been taken care of, the future of the family business needed to be secured. The looming threat was "Aryanisation", Nazi shorthand for confiscation. Business had already become more difficult in 1935, when Jewish-owned companies were excluded from public-sector contracts. Raw material supplies dried up; they were allocated by quota and the factory was cut out. Ernst knew he had to relinquish ownership, but he wanted to ensure the company would keep going. After consulting friends in the business, he engineered a "sale" to an up-and-comer who would be acceptable to the Nazis. Hermann von Müffling fit the bill: as a relative of a famed Prussian field marshal, he had impeccable Aryan credentials – but could not raise sufficient funds to buy the factory, even at a knock-down price. My grandfather arranged a loan of 240,000 Reichsmarks, the equivalent of almost £1.4 million today, borrowing funds from his mother-in-law, presumably knowing that the loan may never be repaid.

Once the sale had gone through, Ernst and Carla needed an exit plan for themselves and for Carla's mother, who lived in a wing of their villa. Towards the end of October 1938, Ernst began writing letters to his business contacts around Europe seeking help. He didn't yet know that he would be arrested just two weeks later, on 9 November, during "Kristallnacht", when the Nazis set fire to the Cottbus synagogue and smashed thousands of shops and other Jewish-owned buildings throughout the Reich. Yet it was obvious they needed to get out of Germany. England was their best hope. "There is little to say about our future," Ernst wrote to a friend in Switzerland. "I am looking for a new country in which to work. I have turned to my friends in England, since England with its cultured and highly developed industry naturally interests me the most." To another contact, the director of an import-export company in Yorkshire who had been a good customer, he wrote: "England is the mother of industry. Do you think, my most esteemed Mr Hodgson, that there might be a company in your country that would be interested in hiring a professional into a management position?"

His correspondents understood the danger even if Ernst wasn't explicit about it. "Herr Frank, the situation is dreadful," Hodgson wrote back. "You are not alone in asking my help, and these requests make me as sad as if you were one of my children." Regretfully, given the depressed state of the apparel sector, finding a position in England could be difficult, he continued. Perhaps Herr Frank might consider moving to South America, for example to Colombia or Bolivia?

Ernst's typed correspondence ends abruptly after his arrest on Kristallnacht. In his absence, my grandmother wrote back by hand. She acknowledged receipt of the letters and asked the senders to be patient. "My husband is not here at the moment and is unable to reply. For that reason, he is particularly interested in your news," she wrote to one English correspondent. Her neat handwriting betrays only a small hint of emotion: she underlined the words "particularly interested" for emphasis.

Ernst was released from jail after ten days. The story Carla later recounted is that the workers at the factory took to the streets to protest his arrest. An academic has found correspondence suggesting that the new factory owner, von Müffling, personally visited the president of the regional council to plead for Ernst's release.[4]

My grandfather's letter writing eventually bore fruit. The owner of a cloth mill in Huddersfield named Frank Broadhead agreed to meet him in Aachen shortly after Christmas and hired him on the spot as his export manager. Leaving Germany took another three months. To obtain permission to leave, Ernst needed an entry visa to England, which in turn required a work permit. In the folder are copies of letters that both Hodgson and Broadhead wrote to the Aliens Department of the UK Home Office, vouching for my grandfather's character and suitability for the job. Eventually, the paperwork was completed. On 21 March 1939, Broadhead sent a cable: "CONGRATULATIONS PERMIT RECEIVED TODAY FURTHER NEWS WILL FOLLOW."

The story of Ernst and Carla's flight to the United Kingdom before it became impossible to leave Germany is exceptional only because they were lucky enough to get out. They lost loved ones, including Ernst's sister, who was murdered in Auschwitz, and almost all their money and possessions, but they survived. My grandparents on my father's side, too, managed to leave in the nick of time in 1938, to the immense relief of my father, who by then was working in London. Other family members were not able to follow suit, including at least five cousins on my father's side who perished in the Holocaust.

Before they could finally leave Cottbus, Ernst, Carla, and Carla's mother still needed to get their confiscated German passports back so that the British consulate could stamp the entry visa. That took one final letter to the Cottbus police and an appearance at the town hall. There, they were obliged to swear an oath never to return to Germany.

How did they feel as they went into exile, leaving a country and a culture that they had considered their own, one that was an essential part of their identity? The most telling clue from the family archives is a speech that Ernst made to the factory workforce announcing the sale of the company. He delivered it just a few days before his November 1938 arrest. It is a speech tinged with sorrow more than anger, one that praises the values and decency of the people who worked with him and soft-pedals the personal trauma. He was stepping down with "a heavy heart", he said, but he was doing so in the knowledge that he had fulfilled his duties to the best of his ability and that the company's traditions and ethics would live on. "Continue to do your duty to this factory, to the new owner, and to your work colleagues," he concluded, "so that in the future the firm can grow and flourish and that honest, proud, and capable people who think justly and act justly continue to work here. That is my parting wish."

2

Role Reversal

Eight decades later, looking back at my grandfather's correspondence and the hope he placed in England as a refuge from tyranny, it is hard to believe we are talking about the same country. The Britain he was so desperate to reach seemed open and generous of spirit, a country that shared his lofty, humanistic values. While there was no shortage of anti-German and anti-Semitic feeling in the UK at the time – on the eve of war – our family was immeasurably helped by the kindness and generosity of many individuals in a way that defined our own views of Britain in the decades that followed. By contrast, the Britain that narrowly voted in 2016 to leave the European Union is deeply divided. There is still much kindness and generosity, but the debate over Brexit quickly became petty, peevish, and – in some quarters – overrun by prejudice. The xenophobia at the heart of Brexit, dressed up as opposition to the free movement of people, is at odds with Britain's self-image as a tolerant and easy-going nation. The idea of "Cool Britannia" may have been part self-delusion; the post-colonial legacy and influx of migrants that took place starting in the 1970s left scars that are easily ripped open. And while London became a thoroughly multicultural city open to the world, the same can't be said for other parts of Britain.

Prime Minister Theresa May's disparagement of "citizens of nowhere" perfectly captured the underlying nastiness of Brexit. That line from her keynote speech at the 2016 Conservative Party conference, four months after the referendum, was an obvious play for populist support from voters feeling unfairly treated and looking for a scapegoat.[5] Some of the grievances are legitimate. The globalisation of the economy over the past three decades has brought multiple benefits, including a level of employment in the UK that hit a record high before the pandemic. However, many have been left behind, as authors from Joseph Stiglitz to David Goodhart have pointed out.[6] Wages have generally stagnated, many jobs have become more precarious, pensions have been cut, and, while some consumer goods like electronics have become cheaper, the cost of housing has soared. Politicians on both the left and right in the UK and in many other advanced economies have largely failed to match the legitimate concerns of ordinary people feeling hard done by with tangible measures to help them. That in turn has spurred growing distrust of authority, deepening pessimism about the future, and political populism. Unfortunately, in the Brexit context, intelligent and factual discussion of topics like immigration and trade quickly degenerated into shouting matches and *ad hominem* attacks fuelled by prejudice. A significant proportion of the media, not just the *Sun* and the *Daily Mail*, gave up any last pretence of journalism to become rabble-rousers, focusing ever more attention and column inches on the "threat" posed by migrants. A study by Oxford University's Migration Observatory shows that the volume of UK press coverage mentioning immigration or migrants more than doubled between 2012 and 2015, and much of it focused either on the volume of arrivals ("mass immigration") or on the problems this supposedly caused.[7] The coverage of Brexit marked a shift in parts of the media to a model of "directed propaganda" similar to that used by Fox News in the United States; in other words, they provided biased and misleading information, or sometimes outright lies, to support a political viewpoint.[8] Even Britain's fabled democracy appeared uncharacteristically wobbly at times, as May's successor, Boris Johnson, first sought to suspend parliament for five weeks during the Brexit debate – an attempt thankfully slapped down by the Supreme Court – and then, in September 2020, presented a bill that deliberately broke international law by violating an agreement on trade with Northern Ireland that the British government had signed with the EU eleven months previously. Even the right to vote is no longer sacrosanct: like many other Britons who have lived outside the UK for years, I was not allowed to vote in the referendum even though my livelihood was directly affected by the outcome.[9]

For most of my life, being British was a source of pride that I had no reason to question. In many ways, I am quintessentially British. I spread Marmite on my toast as a child, became a mediocre cricket player, a devoted Monty Python fan, and a compulsive tea drinker. I thrill to watch British athletes in the Olympics being lauded for their personal best performance, even as they stumble in last. I sing along to *Land of Hope and Glory* at the Last Night of the Proms and am awed by the mastery of the English language and the brilliant subtlety and inventiveness that I continue to find in contemporary British fiction. I like to think that, in my outlook and manners, I espouse the best of British liberalism. I have never lost my English accent, in any language. Yet in regard to Brexit and to the institutional crisis that accompanied it – including my own disenfranchisement – my pride about being British turned to dismay, frustration, and anger, fierce emotions that were assuaged only by the knowledge that many other Britons, including those with more traditional backgrounds, felt the same way. Britain, I feel, has sold out. With Brexit, it turned its back on the core values of tolerance and pragmatic liberalism that have made the country so attractive to so many for so long. By embracing in its stead a narrow and toxic ideology, "Great" Britain belittled itself.

The "citizen of nowhere" jibe felt especially personal. I clearly fit the category of people May was referring to – staunchly pro-European, highly mobile (I now reside in Paris but have lived and worked in many other places including Berlin, Brussels, Copenhagen, Moscow, New York, and Los Angeles), and I am open to the world in all its diversity. Her comment still makes me seethe, years later. Why was my reaction so strong? Reading my grandfather's papers provided the answer. In the disparagement of her tone and in the phrase itself, I heard a personal rejection. I was someone who simply didn't belong in the country I had unquestioningly assumed to be my own. Worse, I could hear echoes of historic name-calling that had vicious and tragic consequences. Here was the modern British equivalent of Stalin's *kulak* and, more personal still, Goebbels' notorious *ewiger Jude*, the grotesque caricature of a "Wandering Jew", which became a staple of Nazi propaganda during the Third Reich.

The role reversal is striking. Britain, the beacon of salvation for my grandparents, has become a place of hand-wringing despair – and the country that has replaced it as the hope-bearer in Europe is none other than Germany. Chancellor Angela Merkel's momentous decision in 2015 to welcome hundreds of thousands of refugees fleeing conflict in the Middle East and Africa sparked dissension within her own country and sharp criticism in other parts of Europe (including in Great Britain). Yet that decision symbolised the decency, tolerance, and respect which have come to characterise Germany today, and which my grandfather called for in his factory farewell speech in 1938. The country has pressing demographic reasons to welcome immigrants, one being its birth dearth over the past few decades, which is already creating shortages of workers. Yet under any circumstances, Merkel's decision was a bold one. And it was accompanied by well-devised integration measures that included expedited processing of asylum requests, language classes, training schemes to raise skill levels, and a concerted effort to find the newcomers work and homes. In Britain in the years between 2013 and 2018, about 213,000 migrants arrived seeking asylum. Germany in the same period took in 1.8 million asylum seekers, more than eight times as many. The Germans needed less than a year to process most of their asylum claims and, within five years, half of them had found gainful employment, including almost 60 per cent of the men. Even given their larger numbers, and their often relatively low skill and educational levels on arrival, a larger proportion of these immigrants found paid work before the pandemic in less time than the previous wave of migrants to Germany from the Balkans during the breakup of Yugoslavia in the 1990s.[10]

The role reversal is manifested in other ways, too. Today,

Berlin is the cool place to be for creative talent. It is Germany that stands up for core democratic values and whose Chancellor does not hesitate to remind Donald Trump of what they are. Indeed, in the understated figure of Angela Merkel, Germany has found a leader who inspires confidence and respect and stays grounded in a crisis. Churchillian she is not, in manners, character, or rhetoric. Yet her low-key but highly efficient approach to problem-solving is just what is needed for today's challenges. Exhibit A for this sweeping statement is Germany's response to the coronavirus crisis. Doubtless helped by Merkel's own background as a scientist, the country moved more quickly to contain the virus and put in place large-scale testing than the UK and other large European countries. The health record speaks for itself: at the time of writing, the United Kingdom's death toll from the pandemic was about four-and-a-half times greater than Germany's, and the difference is even larger when adjusted for population size.[11] German hospitals even used some of their spare intensive-care capacity to take in French and Italian patients. Merkel sought to forge a consensus of state governments in the highly federalised system, which helped gain political approval for the lockdown and subsequent relaxation. Public support reflects that success: polls during the crisis put her popularity as high as 86 per cent.[12] Again, it's striking to note the difference with the UK or countries such as France, where public trust of government action was often lacking. In the UK, people quickly saw through the blustering self-confidence of Johnson and his team: the share of people agreeing that the government was relatively trustworthy dropped precipitously from 67 per cent in April 2020 to just 48 per cent six weeks later.[13]

I don't want to overstate the case; Germany still gets a lot of things wrong. Its empathy and solidarity with the economic and financial plight of other Europeans has limits. In the aftermath of the global financial crisis in 2008, and especially during the Eurozone crisis that followed, Germany came under fierce criticism for "beggar-thy-neighbour" economic policies that forced other European countries to adopt sometimes crushing austerity policies, even as it increased its exports. Here, critics complained, was an example of Germany acting as the selfish leader. The country also has its own political extremists who spew intolerance to foreigners and have gained ground electorally in eastern Germany. The far-right Alternative für Deutschland party won more than 12 per cent of the votes and 94 seats out of 709 in the 2017 parliamentary elections, its best score to date (although its popularity has been waning since). The political clout of these extremists remains of a different order of magnitude to the United Kingdom, where the body politic tripped over itself in the rush to follow the lead of Nigel Farage. Nonetheless, populist extremes continue to lurk in Germany's shadows.

One of the critical and healthy differences with Britain, I think, is that Germany does not reflexively wrap itself in a national flag. Except for when its national team is winning World Cup football games, flag waving is conspicuous by its absence. If anything, given lingering complexes about the overly muscular projection of German power, it shies away from playing a political or diplomatic leadership role that is commensurate with its economic power. The Germans, aptly, have a word for this self-enforced modesty: *Selbstverzwergung*, which literally means turning oneself into a dwarf.

The victorious Allies initially imposed this condition on a defeated Germany in 1945 and, in the 1950s, it became a founding notion of the European Union that West Germany (as it was at the time) should be kept in its place and contained in a peaceful and democratic confederation of neighbouring states. In the context of global security, the old joke about NATO being created "to keep the Americans in, the Russians out, and the Germans down" still rings true. Yet modesty and a certain reserve have become comfortable positions. Germany is at ease as part of a larger Europe. There is no contradiction between being German and being European – quite the opposite: being European has become the essence of being German. The country's very identity, its domestic order, and its own sense of credibility depend on its place at the heart of an integrated continent.

It's easy to criticise this "leadership avoidance complex" – and indeed at times that stance can seem selfish or downright cowardly.[14] Yet it is also understandable, a type of behaviour that suggests a lingering shame about the past, or at least an acute sense of the lessons learned from previous flirtations with national exceptionalism.

Maintaining this stance has, at times, required a delicate balance between German and European interests. The most vivid demonstration of this dates back to 1989, after the fall of the Berlin Wall, as the prospect of German reunification loomed. European leaders meeting in Strasbourg in early December that year, less than a month after the Wall had come down, gave a rough reception to the then German Chancellor Helmut Kohl. In his memoirs, Kohl describes the atmosphere as "more tense and unfriendly" than any other European summit he had ever attended. Margaret Thatcher was bluntly confrontational. Kohl recounts that, over dinner, she said flatly: "We beat the Germans twice, and now they are back."[15] During that meeting, and for years thereafter, Kohl insisted that German unification and deeper European integration were two sides of the same coin. After two days of bad-tempered haggling, the summit ended with a compromise that has shaped Europe's destiny ever since. Germany obtained a declaration on unification that was carefully crafted to take into account Thatcher's opposition. In return, Kohl agreed to the launch of an intergovernmental conference on monetary union the following year as a way of highlighting German commitment to European integration. The meeting marked not so much the birth as the conception of a new European currency, the euro, an idea that was wildly unpopular in Germany at the time. In other words, Kohl essentially sacrificed the Deutschmark for the green light from the rest of Europe to proceed with unification.

As time has passed since reunification, prominent Germans have called for the country to jump over its own shadow. In January 2014, some sixty-nine years after the end of the Second World War, then-German president Joachim Gauck gave a remarkable speech at the annual Munich Security Conference. Gauck is a Lutheran pastor who grew up in the former East Germany and is widely respected as a moral authority; after the fall of the Wall, he ran the agency that reviewed the Stasi's files on millions of East German citizens, a delicate task that required balancing reconciliation with justice. In his Munich speech, he acknowledged that, for understandable reasons, Germany's past weighed heavily on its willingness to be an active participant on the world stage. But for too long it had shirked its duties and responsibilities. There were reasons for the postwar generations of Germans to mistrust German statehood, he said, "but the time of categorical distrust is past". After six decades of living in peace with its neighbours, respecting civil and human rights and the rule of law, and building a vibrant civil society, "we are now permitted to have confidence in our abilities and should trust in ourselves". Germany needed to stop letting others protect its security, prosperity, and freedom, he concluded. It needed not just to live out its values, but to "uphold them together with our friends and partners".[16]

Germany's struggle with itself, its attempt to find the pitch-perfect role that both acknowledges the past and takes into account the reality of the present, has long intrigued me. I followed with interest the so-called *Historikerstreit* that broke out in the 1980s – when a faction of conservative German historians sought to put the Holocaust into a broader historical context in an attempt to relativise its importance. Members of this movement pointed to similarities between the Nazi genocide of Jews and Stalin's brutal persecution of ethnic groups in the Soviet Union, among other comparisons. Such arguments were no less fiercely opposed by other historians who rejected any attempt to "normalise" the Third Reich.[17] I have followed, too, the growing body of contemporary German literature, both fiction and non-fiction, that has sought to make sense of the past for the second, third, and now fourth generations of Germans since the war. That includes some works of stark honesty, as younger generations who were long told that their beloved grandparents passively or actively resisted the Nazis discover that the truth was actually very different, sometimes shockingly so.[18]

My interest in all of this grew from a natural curiosity about Germans and Germany that was not purely academic or theoretical; indeed, it started when I was a child. Of course, my family's roots meant I was perhaps more interested in the issues and certainly more invested in the outcome than someone without the historical connection. Yet the idea that I would one day seek to reclaim our family's German identity and acquire a second passport didn't cross my mind. Why would I want to do so? After all, I had a British passport. That opened all the doors I needed in Europe and around the world. And it was who I was.

Then came Brexit. I happened to be in Croatia on an office retreat with French colleagues on that fateful June day in 2016 when the referendum was held. I heard the result early the next morning. Everyone else heard too. Walking into the hotel dining room for breakfast, they crowded round, curious for my reaction. Dazed, I had only one thought: the vote had made it impossible for me to be both British and European. I told my colleagues: "I feel like I've been orphaned."

3

A New Home

My family knows what it means to be citizens of nowhere. Having been stripped of their German nationality on leaving Germany, my parents and grandparents remained stateless for seven years after they came to England. Their applications to be naturalised as British citizens were routinely rejected during the war, and they received their British papers only nineteen months after it ended.

Once they became British, they never looked back. In the quest for a new life, they downplayed their origins but never quite shook them off. Being born in Germany was baggage, regardless of the circumstances of their departure. After Germany overran the Netherlands, my father was interned along with other male German-born refugees in May 1940. He was first sent to a camp near Liverpool and then to another on the Isle of Man. As he wrote later in his memoir, he chafed at being designated a potential risk: "True, I was born in Germany, but [I] had been deprived of my nationality. I was designated an 'enemy' but I had no more fervent wish than victory for the Allies. I was dubbed an 'alien' when I had just begun to strike fresh roots." The internment lasted five months but he later made light of it, emphasising the intellectual stimulation of being interned with brilliant German–Jewish scholars and artists. For a long time, I had difficulty understanding how he could gloss over these difficult periods in his life, but I have come to see his unbridled optimism and revisionism as a shield that protected him from more violent or sombre emotions.

My parents loved England and felt a deep sense of gratitude. They met in London in the summer of 1944 over tea with mutual friends. "I am fortunate and grateful to have found a girl with whom I have an infinite number of common interests, common views, common likes and common essentials," my father wrote to a close friend. Chief among those points in common were a similar past and a shared vision of the future, as loyal subjects of Her Majesty the Queen. They willingly assumed new identities. We dropped the umlaut in Gümbel, and my father anglicised his first names: Heinrich Eduard became Henry Edward, later just Edward. He successfully passed the British Bar exam in 1941, though he was only officially called to the Bar five years later, after the war, when he became a British citizen. He went on to have a career in the City as an international reinsurance broker. My mother started out in England as a medical orderly, washing bodies in a hospital morgue to earn enough money to live before training as a radiographer. She subsequently gave up her job to raise us, her children. My eldest sister was born in 1948; I'm number four of five. We spoke only English at home. My father attempted *The Times* crossword puzzle every morning on the train to work. Every Sunday, we went to the local Anglican church, where my mother sang in the choir.

In 1951, my father was offered a job in Paris. In those early postwar years, he had at times felt open hostility at work because of his German origin. The timing of the offer made it tempting: he had just been passed over for a promotion. Yet he turned it down. "After all the trauma of leaving Germany I had struck fresh roots in England. We had found a new home in every sense of the word," he wrote. My mother sometimes talked about England as a place she loved because of the "live and let live" mentality. By that, she meant that she felt accepted. They could have easily stayed in London, surrounded by others with similar backgrounds, but they chose to move to a leafy all-England suburb, reconnecting with the comfortable and bourgeois lifestyle they had both enjoyed in Germany before the war. While the neighbours knew or guessed about the family history, most didn't ask questions – at least not directly.

I embraced our family's identity; however, I knew that our Britishness only went so far. My parents spoke excellent English, making only the occasional odd mistake, like confusing "sliver" and "slither", but never lost their soft accent. We almost never went to the pub and, on those rare occasions when we did, it felt like an anthropological field trip rather than a fun lunch out. Home food was different from other people's. My grandmother cooked ox tongue and kohlrabi. At Christmas, we ate *Stollen* fruitcake and almond and cinnamon biscuits shaped like stars or half-moons, called *Zimtsterne* and *Kipferln*. My parents nonetheless felt accepted by their adopted country and, indeed, recognised. In February 1989, the queen awarded my father the Order of the British Empire for services rendered in developing the international insurance market. The pride of that moment shines through in the photos of my parents outside Buckingham Palace after the ceremony. It was a pride we all shared.

In many ways, our family was a poster child for successful immigration and integration. My parents' desire to rebuild their lives in Britain equated with hard work and success, which benefited the country that took us in. My father was not the only one to be decorated by the queen: my aunt was awarded an OBE for her services to radiography at the Middlesex Hospital, where she trained generations of students. Their closest cousins, with whom they had spent many summer holidays in Cottbus as children, were also decorated. One received an MBE for founding a charity that helped handicapped people express themselves through art. Her brother was designated Companion of the Order of the Bath for his work in the Lord Chancellor's Department.

The clearest expression of our willingness to give everything to our new country was of a very different nature: my uncle, the youngest brother of my mother and her twin sister, sacrificed his life. Born Günter but known in the family as Maxi, he had eventually arrived in England on the Quaker-run *Kindertransport* train and boat in 1938, ahead of his parents, Ernst and Carla. My aunt and mother found him a British sponsor family so he could stay in the country rather than have to make the onward trip to Canada. He was just fifteen at the time and determined not to accept his fate passively. As soon as he could, Maxi joined the British army. He enlisted in the No. 3 Troop of the No. 10 Commando, a special unit made up of German–Jewish refugees. As native German speakers, they carried out reconnaissance missions, including in North Africa and Sicily; among other roles, they interrogated captured German officers to obtain intelligence. The existence of the unit was a closely guarded secret to avoid any misgivings or misunderstandings with regular British troops fighting alongside them.[19]

In May 1944, Maxi's unit was parachuted behind enemy lines into Normandy to prepare for the Allied landings, but he was unable to join the mission, having contracted malaria in North Africa. Determined not to be left behind, he joined the heroic D-Day flotilla that crossed the English Channel on 5–6 June. He was killed on the beaches of Normandy as he landed. He is buried in a British military cemetery in Hermanville, near Caen. His gravestone uses his army name: George Mack Franklyn. He was twenty-one.

My grandparents and my mother and aunt were stricken with grief. An abiding memory of my grandmother Carla was the photo of her handsome son in British military uniform that she kept on her bedside table. She would look at us, her grandsons, see a family resemblance, and sigh.

In November 1945, six months after the war ended in Europe, Carla's husband Ernst received a letter from a former industry colleague in Germany. The Cottbus factory had been damaged by Allied bombing raids. Worse, the Soviet authorities who now administered Cottbus were threatening to seize it. Their position had hardened on finding that Herman von Müffling, the man to whom Ernst had "sold" the factory in 1938 to avoid its confiscation, had joined the Nazi party in 1941. The manager's letter contained a plea: in these difficult times for his former home town, would Ernst consider returning to Cottbus to take back the factory? Evidently, by then nobody in Cottbus remembered or cared that Ernst and Carla had been forced to swear an oath on leaving Germany six years previously that they would never go back.

My grandfather refused, firmly. "When I left, I knew for obvious reasons I should never return, a decision which was hardened by the annihilation of my sister in the gas chambers of Auschwitz," he wrote. "The experience we had to go through in 1938 determined my boy to fight for the restoration of humanity and justice with the soldiers of this country, where we enjoyed generous hospitality and nearly unrestricted freedom. His death brought deep grief to us and his undaunted spirit will live with us in this country which was his adopted home."

4

Questions of Nation, Identity, and Mobility

As a student of literature, I have long been interested in how artists and writers who are driven from their homeland can thrive in their changed circumstances. Writers from Ovid and Dante to Rousseau, Joyce, and Kundera produced some of their most powerful work in exile. Victor Hugo, on the run after Napoleon III's 1851 coup, wrote *Les Misérables* in Guernsey. Russian writers have been especially prone to banishment; the list includes Brodsky, Dostoevsky, Nabokov, Pushkin, and Solzhenitsyn.

This experience of exile never resonated with me personally until I moved to Los Angeles in the mid 1990s. There, I started reading the diaries and memoirs of the émigré German artists who flocked to LA in the late 1930s and 1940s, often after an arduous journey that took them through France and across the Pyrenees before they found a ship bound for the United States. Writers, composers, musicians, actors, and philosophers joined this exodus, including Bertolt Brecht, Arnold Schoenberg, Bruno Walter, Theodor Adorno, and the brothers Heinrich and Thomas Mann. They and many others ended up on the west coast, a few with one-year writing contracts from Warner Brothers and Metro-Goldwyn-Meyer, but mostly because the first émigrés to arrive created a welcoming network that attracted the others. The cultural dissonance of these European intellectuals as they discovered both the natural beauty and the intellectual vapidness of Los Angeles life was stark. Two weeks after arriving in Los Angeles in July 1941, Brecht described the city as "a mausoleum of easy going". One strophe in his *Hollywood Songbook* reads: "The town of Hollywood has taught me this / Paradise and hell / can be one city; / For those without means this paradise is hell."

When not mocking their new surroundings or worrying how to make ends meet in a country at war and where most had only a poor grasp of the language and few sources of income, these luminaries spent much of their time thinking, writing, and arguing about Germany, the past, the future, and their own identities as Germans. I was more than intrigued; some of the questions they had asked back in the 1940s were ones that I, too, was asking fifty years later. What had gone wrong? What did it actually mean to be German? Were the atrocities being committed back home an aberration, the grotesque negation of centuries of high German culture and civilisation? Or was there some inherent part of German culture itself that had sown the seeds of the hideous violence and destruction now being wrought in their erstwhile home? Thomas Mann, who wrote his apocalyptic novel *Doctor Faustus* in Los Angeles, famously declared on arriving in the United States in 1938 that, "Wo ich bin, ist Deutschland" – Germany is where I am. The phrase reinforced the notion that Hitler and the Nazis were anathema to "true" Germans, that is, Germans who upheld the values and civilisation of the land of Goethe, Schiller, Bach, and Mendelssohn. Mann's view evolved, however. Seven years later on 29 May 1945 – three weeks after Germany's unconditional surrender – he articulated a darker judgement in a speech delivered at the Library of Congress. "There are not two Germanys, a good one and a bad one," he declared, "but only one, whose best turned into evil through devilish cunning. Wicked Germany is merely good Germany gone astray, good Germany in misfortune, in guilt, and ruin."[20] By then, Mann and his wife, Katia, had become naturalised American citizens.

We can all learn from this intellectual grappling with fundamental questions of identity and what it means to be German, or British, or French, or any particular nationality. In the aftermath of the Brexit vote, I turned back to the diaries, essays, letters, and memoirs of these giants of German literature as potential sources of inspiration and consolation. The situation could hardly be more different, of course. While Britain has set off down a path that I believe to be thoroughly misguided and damaging, it is not a wartime aggressor engaging in atrocities. I live comfortably in Paris, by choice, and have not had to flee for my life. Yet the exercise has been a salutary one – and indeed was one of the sparks for this essay. For as I read through the often mournful writings of these exiles puzzling to understand what had happened to the country they had loved but now grieved over, I admired and began to emulate the contrapuntal narratives they had constructed about the country they felt they had lost, articulating my own questions about Germany and nuancing my hurt feelings about Brexit and the United Kingdom.[21]

Most importantly, their writings made me realise just how much the notion of national identity itself has fundamentally changed in the intervening years.

Where we are born remains an essential part of who we are and how we see ourselves. "Home" starts out as a geographic idea and, even when we move on, our odysseys can become efforts to recover the feeling and comfort of it, no matter where we find ourselves. But first we have to understand what "home" means. With it comes a culture, a language, food, and myriad customs, expectations, and aspirations. Our nationality can shape our other interests, whether they be calligraphy or cricket. For those outside their native countries, whether they are expatriate workers or students spending semesters at universities abroad, finding fellow countrymen and women brings comfort and community. In sports, especially, nationality reigns supreme. A basic tribalism takes over: it goes without saying that English people support the English team, just as the Welsh support Wales, or Scots support Scotland. From a political perspective, as we can see all too clearly, national identity is also an easy rallying cry today. "Make America Great Again" instantly appeals to the reflexive sense of national belonging, complete with the idea that things have gone awry and need to be fixed. Cinemas in England stopped playing *God Save the Queen* before feature films in the 1970s, but it remains *de rigueur* at Wimbledon and international football games. No televised speech by a French president would be complete without the *Marseillaise.* Such long-established rituals and traditions will probably never die. A number of European countries, including Germany and Italy, owe their nationhood to the yearning and struggles for it in the nineteenth century, and the legacy remains powerful. Friedrich Engels famously predicted the "inevitable" withering away of the state, but the nation is a different matter altogether. If anything, the coronavirus pandemic has highlighted just how beholden we remain to national governments and their decisions, however good or erratic, in a time of crisis.

Yet in the second decade of the twenty-first century, my contention is that our identity is more complex and less dependent on our nationality than ever. Our passport is only one aspect of who we are, how we think about ourselves, the way we are viewed by the world, and the characteristics that define us.

The Black Lives Matter protests that erupted worldwide following the videotaped murder of George Floyd in Minneapolis in May 2020 provide one powerful illustration of how issues of identity can and do transcend geography. The protests outside the United States were often tinged by a local agenda; in France, for example, Floyd's death focused renewed attention on the case of Adama Traoré, a Frenchman of Malian extraction who died in police custody in 2016. From Berlin to Tokyo, Floyd was mourned as a victim, a desperate man gasping for breath and calling for his deceased mother in his agony, and as a symbol, a deeply shocking representation of injustice, racial prejudice, gratuitous violence, and hatred. In that sense, he became a Black Everyman. That he happened to have American citizenship is important but not determinant. We identified with his suffering, not his nationality.

There is nothing particularly new about belonging to multiple communities beyond our own narrow national one. Indeed, the social history of the past sixty or so years is the history of personal empowerment and the assertion of multiple identities, from our gender and sexuality to ethnic or religious backgrounds – even dietary habits. In the silent kneeling protest of Colin Kaepernick, the quarterback for the San Francisco 49ers, those old enough to remember can see a flashback to the black-gloved fists raised by US track medallists Tommie Smith and John Carlos during the playing of *The Star-Spangled Banner* at the summer Olympics in Mexico City in 1968.

What has changed is the speed and power with which we now assert our sense of sharing and belonging. The internet is both accelerator and amplifier. Without the video of his murder, or its global dissemination on social networks, George Floyd would have been just another statistic, his tragic death barely noticed outside his immediate family and community. In many other ways, I would argue, the arrival of these technological tools marks a turning point in our lives, speeding the transformation of our idea of self. They enable us to redefine individual identities effortlessly, in a way that transcends national borders and allegiances. It is as if our user IDs and passwords for services like Facebook, Twitter, and Instagram have become as important as our passports, if not more so, in determining who we are and the company we keep.

In the post-geography online world, we are drawn to "like", discuss, or otherwise react with others who have any ethnicity, age, religious belief, or sexual orientation – and who could be anywhere. We visit these networks multiple times a day, for the most part without seeking to shock or confront, in search of information or community, looking for approval to reinforce our own self-esteem or just for amusement.

The young generation of online "influencers" is an example of just how cyberspace has become the new homeland and universality the new flag. Take Valeria Lipovetsky, a former model and mother of three children with a worldwide following of 1.5 million subscribers for her YouTube channel, on which she dispenses fashion, beauty, and nutrition tips. Born in northern Russia, she left for Israel when she was two years old and then moved to Canada at the age of nineteen, where she now lives in Toronto. In one of her videos, she reveals "twenty random facts" about herself. First up: Where are you from? "This is a tricky one," she starts. Even more successful is Felix Arvid Ulf Kjellberg, better known as PewDiePie, a Swedish YouTube pioneer who now lives in Brighton, from where he entertains more than one hundred million subscribers with a mix of comedy, music, and vlogs. If there is one strand that connects this generation of online stars, it is their global presence and outlook.

At the same time, we are seeing a competing trend to this world without borders: the rise of hyper-localism. Local has always been better for some decisions, such as filling potholes. You are suspicious of the ability of the national government to handle the Covid-19 crisis, but – in France, at least – you look to the mayor of your town, village, or *arrondissement* to provide you with face masks. You trust the restaurant manager of the local golf club or burger joint more than the health secretary when it comes to ensuring that you can dine safely. Technology has taken this localism to a new, highly personalised level. Our identities can now be dissected – and manipulated – by biologists based on the sequencing of our genome or by e-commerce sites based on our online browsing habits. Companies like Amazon use their vast data troves about individual preferences to suggest items to us that we as consumers may never otherwise have heard about but which correspond perfectly to our centres of interest. This growing individualisation brings with it a set of risks and threats to our privacy, but it is the opposite of national identity; indeed, it makes it harder than ever to identify characteristics that unite a village let alone an entity as large and diverse as the United Kingdom. Britain is simply a collection of sixty-six million potential shoppers with different preferences.

I used the term "individual identities" in the plural earlier in this chapter because in the virtual world it is easier than ever to have multiple personalities, not in a psychopathological sense but rather in a healthy sense of defining ourselves based on our multiple interests and characteristics. The internet is the great cross-border connector that enables the unencumbered expression of this multiplicity. It links people based on their passions and sense of who they are rather than their nationality, whether it be for golf, chess, vegan recipes, or book collecting. You can be a member of a British-born Chinese food group or an Irish Latvian folk dancing community, or both at the same time.

In this context, patriotism can be another "feel good" community to add to your list of likes. Waving flags online can be charming and fun – when it is innocent. Regrettably, social media is also proving to be a highly effective instrument in manipulating political opinion in the name of national sentiment. The us-versus-them atmosphere that this can create, as we have seen both in Britain and the United States, is not just effective at winning votes, but it can quickly turn poisonous for those labelled as "them".[22] Social networks have for too long allowed themselves to be used as platforms for deliberate political distortion and incitement to hatred (although the excesses of President Trump have forced Twitter and some others to re-examine their standards); while political controversy boosts the revenue of these networks by increasing user engagement – and thus ad spending – it does a broad disservice to society as a whole.

Perhaps I am naive, but I retain my faith in technology's ability to counter such abuses. The transparency and easy dissemination that these platforms provide are also powerful tools in the armoury of democracy and human rights. In the former Soviet Union, political dissidents put themselves in considerable danger to smuggle out *samizdat,* their "self-published" writings that often took months to reach the West. Today, uploading and sharing a video clip or scanned copies of a document takes a matter of minutes at most and reaches a far larger audience instantaneously. Some countries try to block or censor the internet, but the technology is so pervasive that leakages are inevitable. Today, it would surely be impossible to conceal the existence of gulags or extermination camps for very long. Technology is also providing us with ever more sophisticated tools to identify doctored text and images and thus call out "fake" news. Tech firms have a strong self-interest in doing so, to avoid being subject to tougher regulation. If social media had existed back in the days of my grandparents, Goebbels would no doubt have made astute use of bots to turn up the volume even further on Nazi messages of hatred, but other, dissenting voices – including those of Thomas Mann and Bertolt Brecht in exile – would also have been heard in Germany.

Beyond technology and its enabling powers, the evolution towards more complex and multiple identities is both a healthy sign of progress and a return, literally, to our roots. Our age is increasingly mimicking the natural world, where biodiversity is the norm and monocultures the worrisome aberration. Modern agricultural techniques have favoured single cultures of crops such as soy or corn, as they are easier and more economical to cultivate. Yet a large body of scientific literature today highlights the negative effects of monocultures, including the destruction or depletion of soil nutrients, which in turn requires ever larger use of chemicals to replenish them, and leads to high water consumption, increased acidification, and threats to wildlife.[23] And that doesn't include graver environmental effects, such as large-scale deforestation in the Amazon or Indonesia to make way for soy or oil palm trees. Left to its own devices, nature follows a very different path, something closer to a Pareto distribution, with about 20 per cent of crops dominating about 80 per cent of the space or yield, but still leaving room for a range of varieties and species to coexist and flourish together. Politics could learn some valuable lessons here about how diverse societies are healthier than ones that have been artificially kept monolithic. Or rather, politics could relearn some valuable lessons that have been forgotten: already in 1782, the US Congress included the motto *E Pluribus Unum* ("out of many, one") on the Great Seal of the United States, in a neat encapsulation of how diversity creates strength.

*

I was working in Moscow as a journalist for *The Wall Street Journal* when the Berlin Wall came down in 1989, and I stayed there for the next three years, covering the failed coup against the Soviet president Mikhail Gorbachev and the collapse of the Soviet Union. I was in the crowd outside the "White House", the seat of the Russian government, when Boris Yeltsin climbed onto a tank in August 1991 to face down the putschists, an unforgettable moment of political drama. I never completely subscribed to Francis Fukuyama's theory about the "end of history" or the rhetoric about a supposed "new world order", but I certainly shared in the euphoria of the moment. Here was a historic opportunity to move beyond Cold War adversarial greyness, with its twisted logic of mutually assured destruction, to a safer, better, and more prosperous technicolour world.

Looking back over the past thirty years, it's obvious that many things on the global stage haven't changed, or at least haven't changed for the better. International conflicts have not disappeared, countries continue to make territorial land grabs, human rights are still abused, censorship is commonplace, and liberal democracy has not become the global norm; indeed, it is now under attack in many places, including most troublingly in its British and American heartland. Yet the fall of the Berlin Wall perfectly symbolised the critical shift towards a more mobile world in which physical borders still exist but have increasingly lost their meaning. Within Europe, especially, the erosion of geography is a cause of celebration.

Mobility is freedom. Being able to cross from East Berlin to West Berlin, or from Prague to Vienna, unimpeded by high walls, barbed wire, or sentries with machine guns, illustrated that idea starkly.

My grandparents were relatively mobile for their time; in the 1920s and 30s, while still in Germany, they had a car and sometimes drove off for family holidays. I have a few albums with photos of blurry mountain vistas and the just-about recognisable faces of my mother with her sister and brother as children on skis. The new mobility of our era is far more extensive, of course. To some extent, British pioneers of low-cost travel like the airline entrepreneur Sir Freddie Laker were instrumental in driving it forward. A critical date came in 1985, four years before the fall of the Berlin Wall, when negotiators from France, West Germany, and the three Benelux countries met on a riverboat in the Luxembourg town of Schengen and agreed to scrap border controls at their common frontiers. Cross-border mobility had long been an ideal of the postwar European construct and Schengen was its accomplishment, the apotheosis of freedom of movement. In 1995, ten years after the first agreement was signed, the Schengen area was created and now covers twenty-six countries, not only the former Communist nations in Eastern and Central Europe but also non-EU members Iceland, Norway, and Switzerland. Schengen achieved scale: passport and border controls have been dismantled across the continent. For the ordinary traveller, Europe came to resemble a single geographical area more closely than at any time in modern history. We crossed borders that were no longer borders; they existed only on road signs and atlases. For my grandparents, who had to wait anxious months for authorisation to leave Germany, such freedom would have been unimaginable. The same holds for East Germans, Poles, Czechs, Hungarians, and many others who had to wait more than thirty years to taste that freedom.

One of the most jarring – and, frankly, incomprehensible – aspects of Brexit for me is the boast by some British politicians that they have "ended" freedom of movement. It's like being proud that you have ended freedom of speech, something that should actually make you hang your head in shame. Sadly, Britain's historic ambivalence to Europe can often result in own goals like this. Schengen is a case in point. Britain missed out on the opportunity to benefit from the new mobility by clinging to outdated notions of control and opting out of the agreement, even as other, non-EU states opted in. As a result, Britons never got to know borderless borders and thereby never physically felt the difference that being part of Europe can make. Even before the Brexit vote, taking the Eurostar from London to Paris required going through two sets of passport controls at St Pancras, one British and one French, when not even one was really necessary.

Such contradictions highlight the age-old struggle between conflicting visions of Britain as an island apart from Europe and as a country "at the heart" of Europe with a determining role in shaping policy. The contradictions played out even more virulently than usual in the period following the fall of the Berlin Wall, leading to some startling zigzags. One example was the decision by the UK to open its labour market to workers from the new Eastern and Central European member states in 2004 without putting in place a transitional arrangement that most other EU countries insisted on as a way to prevent a sudden influx. The subsequent migration contributed to the rising anti-European and anti-immigration sentiment that became such a critical theme of the Leave campaign.

Covid has brought travel to a near halt, making us appreciate all the more the mobility we took for granted. I have no doubt that this hiatus is temporary and that we will see the return of mobility once the virus has been tamed. For one thing, our prosperity depends on it. The fall of the Berlin Wall coincided with an explosion of cross-border trade in goods, services, and finance that has been an indispensable engine of the global economy ever since. China emerged as a global economic and political power on the back of this movement. More than a billion people worldwide have been lifted out of extreme poverty in the process, according to the World Bank, bringing the total share of the global population still living in extreme poverty down from 36 per cent in 1990 to about 10 per cent today. That is an extraordinary achievement of our time.

We move, a lot. Before the pandemic, 500 million passengers flew across the European Union each year. In 2019, about sixteen million people born in one European country were living in another European country, a sharp increase from just a decade ago. Students are especially mobile: since the Erasmus programme began in 1987–1988, more than three million students in Europe have used it to study in another European country.[24]

How will the United Kingdom fare once it has severed its ties with Europe? Poorly, I suspect. In the 1990s, the country positioned itself brilliantly to capitalise on the mobility revolution and the cross-border flows that were exploding at the time. The City of London fashioned itself as the world's financial centre, and Britain as a whole reaped the benefit; financial services have been the single largest contributor to the UK's surplus in services trade. An important part of London's pull has been its international outlook, with about one in five people working in the City coming from a European country.[25] Manufacturing and services also tapped into the new era with exemplary skill; the British car industry was moribund until it reinvented itself as the manufacturer and assembler of other makers' cars.

Brexit and coronavirus together are too much for any country. My hope is that the pandemic will provide a fresh perspective on what really matters. Already polls suggest a new set of priorities, with health and the economy dominating the list of the most important issues facing Britain. Yet I'm not holding my breath. Brexit has already ripped the fabric of British society. I take no pleasure in seeing the country I was once proud to call home striding off in the wrong direction, but I expect more pain is to come.

5

Taking on Taboos

As the child of German immigrants growing up in England in the 1960s and 70s, I recognise the attitudes that underlie Brexit. I saw and felt them first hand. Being British had many meanings, but one obvious one was the equation of national identity with wartime heroism. The heroism was real, but it became mingled with a misplaced sense of superiority towards and distrust of Europeans in general. In my childhood, Germans bore the brunt of this disdain, and they still largely do. The war comics that boys of my age devoured were replete with the exploits of British commandos as they fought and inevitably killed dastardly "Jerrys". "Take that, *Schweinehund*!" they would cry, lobbing grenades into trenches or slitting throats under cover of darkness. In these comics, Germans were heavyset and ugly, called Fritz or Hans, and prone to shouting nonsense phrases like "*Donner und Blitzen*!"

John Cleese in his Basil Fawlty guise ("don't mention the war") and others have brilliantly lampooned this anti-German obsession. As a child, I saw little to laugh at, however. Instead, I felt a confused sense of shame. Certainly, nothing was to be gained from divulging my German roots, even to friends. When fellow pupils asked me where my father had gone to school, I changed the subject or lied; letting on that he had attended the Stefan George Gymnasium in Bingen would only have subjected me to years of taunting, or so I feared. At the age of sixteen, I brought a girlfriend home for tea. After we left, she wondered about my parents' light accent and asked if they were Dutch. "No, German," I confessed with a mixture of nerves and relief that my secret was finally out. "Oh," she said. We broke up soon after. I blamed my family history, but also wondered whether I was reading too much into it.

At home, too, Germany in general and our family history in particular were subjects to be avoided. That was also the case with our Jewish roots. Yet I was a curious child and started asking questions about who we were and what had happened. There were questions aplenty: why had they not known they were in danger or not reacted more forthrightly? Why had they put aside their Jewish past? Most of all: what had it been like? Such questions received unsatisfactory answers at best, and often no answer at all. One early memory is of a deeply painful conversation around the dinner table when I was eleven years old. I asked my mother directly what she had gone through and why she wouldn't talk about it. She stood up and left the room, shaking with emotion, unable to talk, and in tears. I was filled with guilt and never broached the subject so directly with her again.

Instead, I started digging on my own. I learned German at school and persuaded my father to let me stay with families of his German business contacts during my summer vacations. When my German was good enough, I began to devour contemporary novels by Heinrich Böll and Günter Grass about the wartime and postwar generations. I spent a year at university in Munich as an exchange student and visited all the historic sites, from the monumental Field Marshals' Hall on Odeonsplatz where Hitler had staged his 1923 Beer Hall putsch to the Dachau concentration camp. In those days, a cinema in the centre of town just off Marienplatz showed the 1960 movie version of Goethe's *Faust* every Sunday morning. I saw it eight times, mesmerised and horrified by the brilliant performance of Gustav Gründgens as the demonic Mephistopheles, a role perfectly suited to an actor who had sold his own soul to the Nazis, as described in Klaus Mann's novel *Mephisto*. I became hooked on the Munich opera repertoire of the two Richards – Strauss and Wagner – and ended up writing a dissertation on Wagner's medieval sources for his monumental four-part *Ring* cycle. I discovered Fassbinder movies (*Maria Braun*) and Rilke poetry. In short, I spent the year – and much of my life since – wrestling with the central question of how a country with such a rich humanistic culture could have descended into such barbarity for the twelve years of the Third Reich.

During these years of exploration, I felt instinctively that I was fighting against a deep and unresolved tension within myself. It was a tension that called out for more and better information. As a student and into my twenties, I devoured a library of books and articles about the Holocaust and especially about how the "second generation", the children of survivors, tend to absorb some of the psychological burdens of their parents. Much of it is written by Israeli psychiatrists based on first-hand studies.[26] My relief at this discovery was palpable: I was not alone. I empathised very deeply with some, but by no means all, of the symptoms described in the literature, especially the overdeveloped search for meaning, the often nebulous feelings of guilt and, most especially, the frustrating lack of intergenerational communication. It was as though a locked box of emotion were deeply embedded within me. Trying to open it, trying to pierce that guilt-laden silence, felt both perilous and liberating.

The breakthrough came at university. One day in my second year, I plucked up the courage to divulge my family background to my flatmates, my closest friends. To my surprise and delight, far from turning their back on me, as I had feared, they were curious and encouraging. If anything, they told me, my openness was endearing for being so hesitant.

If my parents had misgivings about my exploration of all things German, they did not let on. Indeed, as they grew older, they became more reconciled with their country of origin. This was especially true for my father, whose business often took him to Germany. There he helped rebuild Anglo–German ties in insurance and, in 1984, five years before being decorated by the queen, he was awarded the German Order of Merit for his services. He collected the decoration from the German Ambassador in London. He was more willing than my mother to talk about the past and spent the last months of his life writing his memoirs, although even then he remained circumspect about many of the details and emotions. The issue became a live one for my mother again after the fall of the Berlin Wall, when her family regained possession of the Cottbus villa where Ernst and Carla Frank, her parents, had lived. It was part of a restitution settlement which also paid compensation for the since-destroyed cloth factory. In a gesture of reconciliation, she and her cousins, who had also settled in England, decided to use the money to set up a charitable foundation to sponsor the theatre and the university in

Cottbus. In doing so, they closed a circle of history in their own way, continuing a tradition of patronage in the town that had been started by their grandparents. She nonetheless avoided talking about her German past and was deeply uncomfortable about it, even in her final years.

Germany, too, has evolved and taken on its taboos. We are now into the fourth generation since the war. Germans today laugh at the ridiculous portrayal of Nazi villains in *Hogan's Heroes* no less than people in other countries do. They also keep their cool when other Europeans fall back on Nazi stereotypes to reproach them, as the Greeks did during the Eurozone crisis of 2012 – and as the British did during and after the Brexit campaign. Barbed comparisons poured forth: Nigel Farage described Brexit as akin to the "Great Escape", the mass breakout of British prisoners of war from the Nazi prison camp Stalag Luft III. The *Mail on Sunday* splashed a story about how Merkel's "attack dog" (in reality, the chairman of the German parliament's EU affairs committee) was supposedly threatening Britain with a trade war, under the headline, "Germans: 'You can't survive without us'". The article quoted a Tory MP, Bill Cash, as saying, "Britain [fought] Germany in two world wars to keep its freedoms and [is] not going to surrender them to a German-run Brussels now."[27] More crudely still, the Leave EU campaign tweeted a photo of Merkel with her arm raised, suggesting a Hitler salute, with the caption: "We did not win two World Wars to be pushed around by a Kraut."[28] On the BBC and elsewhere, the plucky spirit of the Blitz was frequently evoked as being able to carry the country through any hardship that Brexit (and, later, the coronavirus) may cause.

The insults speak volumes about the immaturity of those hurling them and nothing at all about the reality of today's Germany. Spending time in that country with an open mind, as I have tried to do, it is impossible to ignore the ever-present and, I believe, sincere emotions behind German penitence for its past. The former German president Richard von Weizsäcker expressed them most eloquently more than three decades ago in his 1985 speech to the Bundestag marking the fortieth anniversary of the war's end in Europe. "The vast majority of today's population were either children then or had not been born. They cannot profess a guilt of their own for crimes that they did not commit," Weizsäcker said. "All of us, whether guilty or not, whether old or young, must accept the past." His conclusion: "Let us face up as best we can to the truth."

In May 2020, on the seventy-fifth anniversary, President Frank-Walter Steinmeier followed up with his own, updated version of that speech. 8 May 1945 was indeed a day of liberation for Germany, he acknowledged, but "it has taken three generations for us to admit it wholeheartedly." The country first needed to go through "an internal liberation, a long and painful process which involved facing up to the past, investigating what people knew and what they had colluded in. Raising painful questions within families and between the generations. Fighting to stop silence and denial from prevailing. It took decades – decades in which many Germans of my generation gradually learned to find their peace with this country."

For all these fine words, ugliness has not been banished forever. I discovered that for myself in 2019, when I received an urgent email from a cousin who lives in Germany. A developer in the Rhineland-Palatinate town of Albisheim was about to knock down a timber-framed house built by my father's ancestors in 1704; local authorities apparently didn't see any reason to preserve the historic "Gümbelhaus" despite vigorous last-minute interventions by my cousin, who argued that it was a monument to the town's Jewish history. Yet this sort of action, in my experience, is an exception; elsewhere, I have found an abundance of the spirit of remembrance and atonement to which Steinmeier referred. I spent two years in Berlin in the mid-1990s for the *Wall Street Journal* and was intrigued to find a city struggling to reinvent itself. Berlin is a particular haven of tolerance, which it learned during the Cold War when it was divided by the Wall and, in the Western part, at least, became a city of draft dodgers and war widows. In today's Berlin, you continue to trip over history, sometimes literally. Both there and in many other towns in Germany, paving stones with the names of Jewish families who were deported to their deaths mark the streets in front of houses where they once lived.

My own move from reconciliation with the past to actually requesting German citizenship required a leap nonetheless. I was British and Britain was part of Europe. What need could I possibly have for a second European nationality? Then came Brexit. I had immediate practical concerns: without an EU passport, I would need a permit to continue living and working in France. If, one day, I wanted to switch to another European country, that could be difficult, too. Yet such practical considerations were only one part of the story. If the issue for me had simply been to acquire another European passport,

I could have just as easily applied for a French one, given that I have been a resident in Paris since 2002. Seeking German naturalisation was a bigger decision altogether. It was a way to counter the shock of being orphaned by the Brexit vote.

The government office in Cologne that deals with these naturalisation cases took almost two years to process the application. On the day I picked up my citizenship certificate at the Paris consulate, I felt a mild euphoria. Eighty years of formal estrangement were ending. I had expected some sort of ceremony, but there was none. My daughter and I just signed some papers, a polite consular official countersigned, and that was it. We were soon outside again.

More than a year later, I still feel lucky and, indeed, privileged. Having a second passport that allows me to maintain my freedom of movement across Europe is a great luxury, and one for which I am grateful. My European credentials are, in fact, stronger than ever: my partner is French, from a family with deep Catholic roots. Generations of her ancestors fought against the British and did so with such heroism during the Hundred Years War that Charles VII of France (1403–1461) gave the family a noble title, the first of several bestowed on them over the centuries. France's battles against the neighbour to the east were also frequent; both of her grandfathers were taken captive in Germany during the Second World War. My life is thus truly multicultural, multilingual, multi-faith, and anchored in European culture and history. Best of all, today that's just fine in a way that would have been unthinkable for my grandparents and the generations before them.

6

Citizens of Everywhere

After the war, my grandmother Carla got back in touch with a select few friends and acquaintances in her former German hometown of Cottbus. One was Willi Zehe, a manager in the family factory who had helped Carla and her husband fill out the reams of paperwork the Nazis had thrown at them as they were leaving in 1939, including a list of extortionate tax demands for both the factory and their household. In 1953, Carla wrote to Zehe with considerable frankness. "How many years did your generation waste so unnecessarily?" she asked. "I pray to heaven so often that the coming generation may be spared that. If that is not the case, we simply cannot enjoy our grandchildren without worrying about them."

She was writing as Cold War tensions were growing and after the death of her husband, Ernst, but she need not have worried; we, her grandchildren, have not had to experience persecution, war, or any of the hardships that she did. Will *our* children and grandchildren be so fortunate? The world of transparency and mobility that I embrace is far larger than just Britain, Germany, France, or even Europe. Yet looking around the globe, it is easy to feel despondent. I am now almost the same age as my grandmother was when she wrote that letter. I sometimes wonder whether I am deluding myself by thinking that openness to the world is not only possible but essential. Many countries, including the United States, have been moving in the opposite direction. We have learned in the past few years that facts don't matter. Our age of mobility is also an age of untruth, an age in which perception and propaganda have gained the upper hand.

In that regard, we have moved back to a much darker era. It is described, chillingly well, by the Austrian writer Stefan Zweig, in his autobiography *Die Welt von Gestern* (*The World of Yesterday*). He opens with a reflection on his childhood in Imperial Vienna before the First World War, in what seemed at the time to be a golden age of rising prosperity and technical advances. Electric light had replaced gas lamps, and the automobile was the new-fangled form of transportation. Poverty and hunger were being vanquished. "We looked back with scorn at earlier periods, with their wars, famines, and revolts," Zweig wrote. "Now it was just a matter of decades before evil would be overcome once and for all. The faith in this period of unbroken and unstoppable progress had the power of religion; we believed in this progress more than in the Bible, and its Gospel seemed to be proven daily by new scientific and technical wonders."[29]

The book was published posthumously after Zweig and his wife died by suicide in Brazil in 1942. Having set us up in the seemingly safe world of his childhood, he spends the rest of the work describing the terrifying descent into loss of empire, fascism, and, subsequently, the mass destruction of human lives in the two world wars and the Holocaust, "the eruption of collective bestiality," as Zweig calls it. Evil had not been overcome, far from it.

Could we again sink back into madness today, in the first half of the twenty-first century? There are some troubling parallels in Zweig's writing between the technological progress, the burgeoning trade, and the spirit of progress that he describes back in his childhood and our pre-Brexit, pre-coronavirus world. Do these hopeful advances merely conceal newly vicious tendencies that threaten our lives and livelihoods? I don't believe so – but then, neither had Zweig. Nor had my grandparents in Germany in the 1930s: from my grandfather's correspondence, it is clear that they hadn't thought they could be in danger until they were.

Today we can note and fret about the risks facing our liberal democracies, but we cannot measure those risks or know how much they will grow. All the more essential, then, for us to fight for the most important principles that are under threat: the principles of diversity, of tolerance, and of openness. We must combat the propaganda and the lies about immigration and its supposedly negative effects. We must fight for historical truth. We must fight to keep borders open and to pull down walls. Our precious freedom to move is still fragile and not shared everywhere. Those of us lucky enough to have it must guard it with especial care, expose those who would destroy it as charlatans and drive them out with vigour and determination.

*

My grandmother's prayer in 1953 was answered. She was able to love and spoil her grandchildren, and her first great-grandchildren, without worrying about a return of fascism. She died in September 1989 at the age of ninety-nine. Had she lived six weeks longer, she would have witnessed the fall of the Berlin Wall. I have no doubt that she would have rejoiced along with the rest of us.

She and my parents, in their own complicated ways, transmitted to me a raw bundle of facts and omissions, emotions, and silences about what they lived through. We as a family are still working through them. Now it is our turn to pass on that heritage to our own children and the next generations. President Steinmeier's "internal liberation" needs to continue – not just in Germany, but in my own family, too.

My daughters, both in their early twenties, have no complexes about the past. They have not had to prise open any locked boxes or come to terms with transmitted feelings of shame and guilt. Born in the United States, they grew up in Paris with three passports, none of which happens to be French. They are who they are and identify themselves as they choose, without any of the inhibitions that I felt growing up. They are citizens of everywhere. "Where are you from?" is not a question they fear. Their cultural, national, and linguistic diversity is something to celebrate, something that gives them an edge, not something to be buried. We have no taboo subjects about who we are and where we come from. Yet whether they want to be or not, the next generation will be actors in the drama that is playing out around us, both witness and evidence of the benefits of openness. They personify freedom of movement as they live, work, and study around the world, the first generation able to do so with ease. It is an extraordinary freedom, and it is important that they are not the last to enjoy it.

My elder daughter, who accompanied me to the German consulate in September 2019 to pick up our naturalisation certificates, was happy to add another passport to her collection, a fourth. She was largely unfazed by the historical significance of it all. As we left the consulate, she stopped to take photos for Instagram. She told me that a German passport "is one of the best you can have," and promptly googled it to prove her point. Sure enough, on a list of the "most useful" passports in the world, Germany ranks second, just after Japan and Singapore. Britain comes sixth. The criteria for the rankings struck me as open to question, but no matter. Being German is cool again, and that's a good development. What matters to me is that she and her sister make full use of their freedoms and that their generation fights to preserve them and extend them to others. They are the generation that now must carry the flame not just for freedom of movement but also for tolerance, universal values that were so precious for my grandparents and so essential for our family's survival. And this generation must do so at a time when planetary threats suddenly seem larger than ever. Not being caught up in a claustrophobic web of national allegiances is an encouraging first step. Let nobody ever need ask, as my grandmother once did, how many years they wasted unnecessarily.

As for me, I am still English but now I am also German, and learning to be proud of that, too. Becoming German has actually provided me with a new perspective on Britain and the Brexit vote. I am still saddened, but I am less angry. I can hear and see the counterpoints more clearly, with less of a rush of emotion. I have even started using my new German passport and identity card, although I admit that it still feels a little strange. The first time was when I checked into a hotel in Berlin in January 2020, one of my last journeys before the Covid lockdowns. The receptionist reflexively spoke English to me. I handed over my German ID and she looked at me with surprise. I smiled and switched to German.

Notes

1 The section of the German Basic Law (Grundgesetz) pertaining to restored citizenship is Article 116, paragraph 2.

2 Documents detailing the couple's charitable activities are in the Cottbus city archive. See Steffen Krestin, "Dem Andenken Max Grünebaums gewidmet", *Cottbuser Blätter*, 2000.

3 See for example Marion Berghahn, "The Process of Jewish Assimilation in Germany", In *German-Jewish Refugees in England,* Palgrave Macmillan, 1984, and David Bronsen (ed.), *Jews and Germans from 1860 to 1933, The Problematic Symbiosis,* Reihe Siegen, 1979.

4 Beatrix Heintze, *Walter Cramer, die Kammgarnspinnerei Stöhr & Co. in Leipzig und die sogenannte "Judenfrage"*, Leipzig, 2003.

5 May gave her speech at the Conservative Party conference in Birmingham on 5 October 2016. The relevant passage reads: "Today, too many people in positions of power behave as though they have more in common with international elites than with the people down the road, the people they employ, the people they pass in the street. But if you believe you're a citizen of the world, you're a citizen of nowhere. You don't understand what the very word 'citizenship' means."

6 Joseph Stiglitz, *Globalization and its Discontents*, W.W. Norton, 2002; David Goodhart, *The Road to Somewhere: The Populist Revolt and the Future of Politics*, Hurst & Co Publishers, 2017. Other powerful books on the topic include Amy Goldstein, *Janesville: An American Story*, Simon and Schuster, 2017, and J. D. Vance, *Hillbilly Elegy: A Memoir of a Family and Culture in Crisis,* HarperCollins, 2016.

7 *A Decade of Immigration in the British Press*, The Migration Observatory, University of Oxford, November 7, 2016.

8 I borrow the term "directed propaganda" from Simon Wren-Lewis, an emeritus professor of economics at Oxford, who used it in his *Mainly Macro* blog in a 6 May 2020 post titled "Why the media in UK and US has moved beyond manufacturing consent, and why that has led to a war about reporting COVID-19". An analysis by the Reuters Institute for the Study of Journalism of media coverage of the 2016 referendum found that, after factoring in the reach of different newspapers, 48 per cent of all referendum-focused articles were pro-Leave, while 22 per cent favoured Remain. David A. L. Levy, Billur Aslan, and Diego Bironzo, *UK Press Coverage of the EU Referendum*, Reuters Institute for the Study of Journalism, 2016.

9 I was one of an estimated two million UK citizens living abroad not allowed to vote in the referendum because we had been out of the country for more than fifteen years, a threshold which the Conservative government itself defined as "arbitrary" in the 2015 Queen's Speech.

10 For details of the successful measures to integrate asylum seekers in Germany, see Herbert Brücker, Yuliya Kosyakova, and Eric Schuß, *Fünf Jahre seit der Fluchtmigration 2015*, Institut für Arbeitsmarkt und Berufsforschung, 4/2020.

11 Data on coronavirus deaths from Johns Hopkins University's online Coronavirus Resource Center, retrieved on 28 September 2020.

12 ZDF Politbarometer, 10 July 2020.

13 *Trust in UK Government and News Media COVID-19 Information Down, Concerns Over Misinformation from Government and Politicians Up*, Reuters Institute for Study of Journalism, 1 June 2020.

14 For a description of the leadership avoidance complex, see Simon Bulmer and William E. Paterson, *Germany and the European Union: Europe's Reluctant Hegemon?* Red Globe Press, 2020.

15 Helmut Kohl, *Erinnerungen 1982–1990*, Droemer Knaur, 2005. Thatcher did not hide her hostility to German reunification; for example, she bluntly told President Gorbachev on a visit to Moscow that Britain did not support it. See Michael Binyon, "Thatcher told Gorbachev Britain did not want German unification", *The Times*, 11 September 2009.

16 Joachim Gauck, "Germany's role in the world: Reflections on responsibility, norms and alliances", opening speech to Munich Security Conference, Munich, 31 January 2014.

17 For a useful summary of the personalities and arguments, see Gordon Craig, "The War of the German Historians", *New York Review of Books*, 15 February 1987.

18 See for example, Harald Welzer, Sabine Moller, and Karoline Tschuggnall, *"Opa war kein Nazi": Nationalsozialismus und Holocaust im Familiengedächtnis*, Fischer, 2002.

19 The story of the commando unit is best recounted in a book by one of its members, Peter Masters, *Striking Back: A Jewish Commando's War Against the Nazis*, Presidio Press, 1997.

20 Hans Rudolf Vaget, *Thomas Mann, der Amerikaner*, S. Fischer, 2011.

21 Various scholars have noted the duality that springs from banishment, which can lead to a form of "contrapuntal" perception that weaves together the real and the imaginary, the old and the new, the living and the dead. See Edward Said, *Culture and Imperialism,* Vintage, 1993, and Michael Seidel, *Exile and the Narrative Imagination*, Yale University Press, 1986.

22 For linkages between often manipulated social media posts and the Brexit vote, see Yuriy Gorodnichenko, Tho Pham, and Oleksandr Talavera, *Social Media, Sentiment and Public Opinions: Evidence from #Brexit and #USElection*, NBER Working Paper 24631, May 2018; Max Hänska and Stefan Bauchowitz, "Tweeting for Brexit: How social media influenced the referendum", in: John Mair, Tor Clark, Neil Fowler, Raymond Snoddy, and Richard Tait (eds.), *Brexit,*

Trump and the Media, Abramis Academic Publishing, 2017.

23 See for example Qingyun Zhao et al., "Long-term Coffee Monoculture Alters Soil Chemical Properties and Microbial Communities", *Nature*, April 2018, and Miguel A. Altieri, "The Ecological Impacts of Large-scale Agrofuel Monoculture Production Systems in the Americas", *Bulletin of Science, Technology & Society*, University of North Florida, April 2009.

24 Eurostat, *People on the move – statistics on mobility in Europe*, 2020 edition.

25 "Record number of European workers in the City of London", City of London press release, 29 January 2018.

26 For a useful overview, see Natan P. F. Kellermann, "Transmission of Holocaust Trauma – An Integrative View", *Psychiatry*, Fall 2001, number 64, issue 3.

27 *Mail on Sunday*, 13 February 2016.

28 The tweet was later deleted by the Brexit campaign group after condemnation by cross-party MPs. Arron Banks, the co-founder of Leave EU, acknowledged that the group "went too far". The anti-German rhetoric stirred up by the Brexit referendum marked a change from the friendlier tone adopted by some tabloids a few years previously. For example, in July 2014, after Germany won the World Cup, the *Daily Mirror* published an article with the headline "Official: It's cool to be German now – and it's okay to love them too".

29 The author's translation of the German original. Stefan Zweig, *Die Welt von Gestern*, Fischer Taschenbuch Verlag, December 2011, page 17.

HAUS CURIOSITIES

Inspired by the topical pamphlets of the interwar years, as well as by Einstein's advice to 'never lose a holy curiosity', the series presents short works of opinion and analysis by notable figures. Under the guidance of the series editor, Peter Hennessy, Haus Curiosities have been published since 2014.

Welcoming contributions from a diverse pool of authors, the series aims to reinstate the concise and incisive booklet as a powerful strand of politico-literary life, amplifying the voices of those who have something urgent to say about a topical theme.

'Nifty little essays – the thinking person's commuting read'
– *The Independent*

Britain in a Perilous World: The Strategic Defence and Security Review We Need
by Jonathan Shaw

The UK's In-Out Referendum: EU Foreign and Defence Policy Reform
by David Owen

Establishment and Meritocracy
by Peter Hennessy

Greed: From Gordon Gekko to David Hume
by Stewart Sutherland

The Kingdom to Come: Thoughts on the Union Before and After the Scottish Referendum
by Peter Hennessy

Commons and Lords: A Short Anthropology of Parliament
by Emma Crewe

The European Identity: Historical and Cultural Realities We Cannot Deny
by Stephen Green

Breaking Point: The UK Referendum on the EU and its Aftermath
by Gary Gibbon

Brexit and the British: Who Are We Now?
by Stephen Green

These Islands: A Letter to Britain
by Ali M. Ansari

Lion and Lamb: A Portrait of British Moral Duality
by Mihir Bose

The Power of Politicians
by Tessa Jowell and Frances D'Souza

The Power of Civil Servants
by David Normington and Peter Hennessy

The Power of Judges
by David Neuberger and Peter Riddell

The Power of Journalists
by Nick Robinson, Barbara Speed, Charlie Beckett and Gary Gibbon

Drawing the Line: The Irish Border in British Politics
by Ivan Gibbons

Not for Patching: A Strategic Welfare Review
by Frank Field and Andrew Forsey

Fiction, Fact and Future: The Essence of EU Democracy
by James Elles

A Love Affair with Europe: The Case for a European Future
by Giles Radice

Integrity in Public Life
by Vernon White, Claire Foster-Gilbert and Jane Sinclair

The Responsibilities of Democracy
by John Major and Nick Clegg

'We Are the People': The Rise of the AfD in Germany
by Penny Bochum

Secret Service: National Security in an Age of Open Information
by Jonathan Evans

Truth in Public Life
by Vernon White, Claire Foster-Gilbert and Jane Sinclair

The London Problem: What Britain Gets Wrong About its Capital City
by Jack Brown